BRITAIN IN OLD PHOTOGRAPHS

HENLEY-ON-THAMES
PAST & PRESENT

JOHN PILLING &
LORRAINE WOODS

SUTTON PUBLISHING LIMITED

OXFORDSHIRE BOOKS

Sutton Publishing Limited
Phoenix Mill · Thrupp · Stroud
Gloucestershire · GL5 2BU

XFORDSHIRE BOOKS

First published 2000

Title page photograph: At the Henley Royal
Regatta, 1890s.

British Library Cataloguing in Publication Data
A catalogue record for this book is available from the
British Library.

ISBN 0-7509-2438-1

Typeset in 10.5/13.5 Photina.
Typesetting and origination by
Sutton Publishing Limited.
Printed and bound in England
by J.H. Haynes & Co. Ltd, Sparkford.

Looking into Bell Street from the Market Place, *c.* 1919. Henley appears to be slumbering on a warm summer's afternoon and traffic queues are not a problem. The shop on the corner is Timothy White's Cash Chemists, which survived on this site until 1984. (*Henley Standard*)

CONTENTS

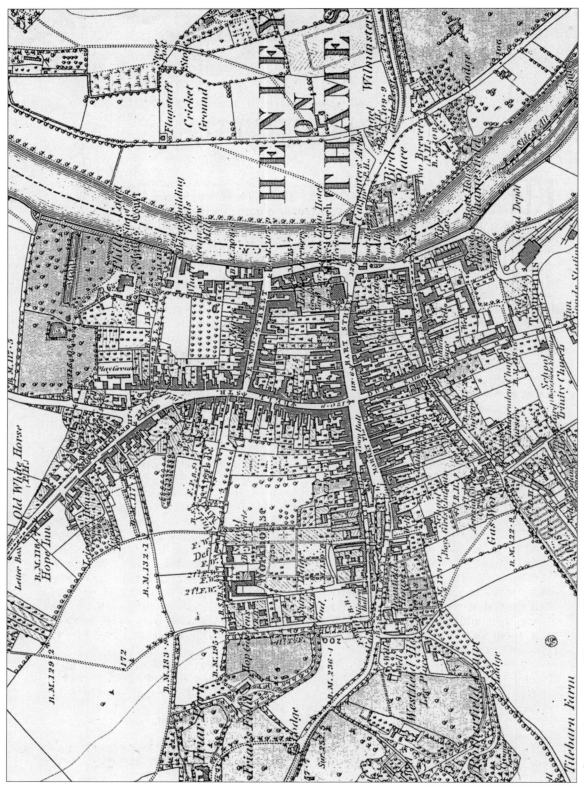

Ordnance Survey map of Henley, 1884.

INTRODUCTION

Henley-on-Thames is no ordinary riverside town. Its name conjures up an image in people's minds across the world of the fashionable elite at leisure, of affluent living and of rowing at its best. Henley has made a name for itself.

However, the pictures in this book show that this was not always so. Many of the early photographs in this book show shabby and poorly kept houses, empty warehouses and muddy and ill-paved streets. Henley had reached the nadir of its fortunes following the building of the Great Western Railway from London to the west of England in the 1840s, which had taken much of the town's livelihood with it. The traffic and trade that had once passed through the town by river and road had now been taken by the new railway. Reading, Didcot and Swindon prospered as Henley fell into recession.

Henley grew up as a river port and its origins can be traced back to the early twelfth century. Barges used to moor along wharves on the river banks to load up with corn, malt, building stone and timber for onward shipment to London and beyond, whilst incoming barges brought luxuries from the metropolis to be unloaded on to pack horses. Stone for the building of Eton College, for example, was transported overland to Henley for shipment downstream, and barges named after local pubs such as the *Angell* and the *Rose and Crown* carried barley from the rich surrounding agricultural land to London. As the town prospered, a bridge was built across the Thames close to where the modern bridge now stands, and streets were laid out in a grid pattern. Even as recently as 200 years ago the majority of Henley's population was dependent on the river trade, working either on the wharves or in associated occupations such as boat-building and as inn-keepers.

During the eighteenth century Henley became a convenient stopping place for coaches and carts travelling between London and the west using the new turnpike roads. Old inns such as the Bull Inn in Bell Street and the White Hart in Hart Street took on a new lease of life, and others were rebuilt in a grander style such as the Red Lion and the Angel, both well situated by the bridge at the entrance to the town. The stagecoach and Royal mail services reached their peak in the 1830s and travellers to London, for example, had the choice of the *Royal Mail* and *Rocket* from the White Hart, the *Coach* from the Red Lion and the *Regulator* from the Black Bull. When the bridge had to be rebuilt in 1786 following the destruction of the old one in a flood, it was constructed with carved stonework and balusters to reflect a new sense of pride felt by the townspeople, and ten years later the old Market House and Guildhall were swept away to make room for a Town Hall. Henley remained a small town, however, and by 1838 its population had reached only about 4,000.

The opening of the Great Western Railway to Reading brought about a sudden collapse in Henley's river and road trade. When James Thorn visited the town in 1847, he felt compelled to write in his *Rambles by Rivers*, that 'there are several large inns, to which was formerly a considerable posting trade attached, but that it was almost destroyed by the railway'. Although a branch link with the main line at Twyford was established in 1857, Henley had lost out in the railway age.

The town had to find itself a new living. Residents remembered how many visitors had come to the town in 1829 when the University Boat Race was held on their stretch of the Thames, and they decided to stage their own one-day event in 1839. A number of regattas followed but most were not an outstanding success, especially after other riverside towns such as Maidenhead and Marlow began to organise their own competing events. However, the patronage of Prince Albert in 1851 and the opening of the railway in 1857 gave the regatta a new impetus, and by the end of the century it had become firmly established in the English calendar of social events and was attracting crews and spectators from throughout the world. The regatta is held during the twenty-seventh week of the year, usually the first week of July, and its very success is now causing concern among residents of the town. Over 50,000 visitors to a town of about 12,000 people can cause major problems, not least on the roads where 9 mile queues during Regatta Week are not unknown.

The Regatta put Henley on the map for the country's social elites, and this, combined with its splendid setting in the Thames Valley, soon attracted visitors and permanent residents alike. Travel time by train to Paddington had been reduced to a little over an hour by 1900 and it was now possible to commute daily to a city office, as it was also possible to make a day trip to Henley from London or Reading. A new prosperity had begun to revive the town's spirits and many of the photographs in this book reflect this new self-confidence and pride. Luxury hotels such as the Imperial were built to accommodate fashionable visitors, builders and hirers of pleasureboats such as H.E. Hobbs and Sons acquired new premises, grand mansions in large grounds were springing up and streets of terraced houses were being erected to house those employed in an expanding range of service industries.

Large employers have never dominated the town, but brewing and malting have long been Henley's main industries. Good quality barley was grown in the surrounding area and much of it was either malted before being loaded on to barges for London, or was consumed by the several local breweries. Pigot and Co.'s Street Directory of 1823 lists twelve maltsters and in the 1850s five breweries are known to have been in business in the town. When W.H. Brakspear and Sons bought out its rival, Greys of Friday Street, at the end of the nineteenth century, it became the sole survivor and remains so today.

Henley in the twentieth century has avoided the wholesale redevelopment that has robbed many other towns of their identities, but having built prosperity on its reputation as a desirable place to visit and live, it knows that this reputation must not be put in jeopardy. The photographs show a remarkable continuity in the fabric of the town and in the conservation of the surrounding countryside, but change has not been altogether absent. Many of the individual shops seen in the old photographs have been replaced by chain stores, and the controversial development by Waitrose supermarket has changed the look of many town centre streets for ever. Other buildings have retained much of their external appearance but have been adapted for new uses, for example as offices for state-of-the-art business in the financial services sector, or as luxury homes for commuters and the retired. The greatest change, however, can be seen on the streets themselves, in the form of the cars and lorries that now congest the town and the road markings and signs that are necessary for their control. The trial traffic scheme introduced in 1999 is the latest attempt to recapture the more congenial atmosphere for pedestrians and shoppers that characterise the pictures taken 100 years ago, but the mixed reception it has received reflects the complexity of modern traffic problems.

The photographs in this book bring out both the change and the continuity. The old photographs draw on the work of several professional photographers, including Jules Guggenheim of the Market Place, Frederick Johnson of Duke Street, William Marshall of 31 Hart Street and George Bushell of 37 Hart Street, as well as the extensive collections left by Oxford photographer Henry Taunt (1824–1922). Other photographs have been selected to illustrate Henley in the middle years of the twentieth century. The new photographs to match the old were taken by Lorraine Woods in 1999 and 2000, and they will no doubt induce the same sense of amazement in future generations as those one-horse pictures of the 1880s do in us.

CHAPTER ONE

HART STREET & THE MARKET PLACE

Hart Street looking towards St Mary's Church on a market day, *c.* 1887. Most of the carts in this picture seem to have been parked for the day and one assumes that the horses have been put out to graze on a nearby meadow.

The Market Place when every available space was filled with parked cars, 1950s. (*River and Rowing Museum, Henley-on-Thames*)

Opposite: The town centre today looks much quieter here following the introduction of a trial pedestrianisation scheme in January 1999. Following amendments to the scheme in September 1999, some west-bound traffic has been re-admitted to one side of the Market Place but aspects of this latest attempt to solve Henley's traffic problems remain controversial. The walled precinct with trees was completed in 1974 and named Falaise Square in honour of Henley's French twin town.

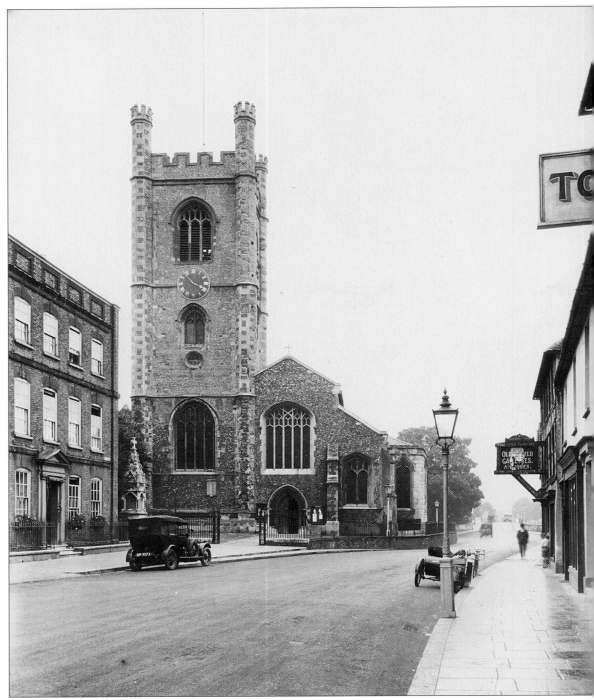

St Mary's Church stands proudly by the bridge over the Thames and has always been a landmark in Henley. It
origins go back to the early thirteenth century and the tower, with its decorative flint and stone facing, is said to
have been built by John Longland, Bishop of Lincoln in 1521–47. This photograph was taken in 1927, and
includes some delightful cast-iron lampstands and a couple of period cars.

The scene has not changed greatly except for the loss of the railings in front of the church door, and the road markings.

St Mary's Church from the end of the bridge, *c.* 1885. The walls of the early sixteenth-century Lady Chapel show their attractive chequer pattern construction in flint and stone, and in the foreground the brick archway leads to the Red Lion Hotel, which is shaded behind an enormous tree.

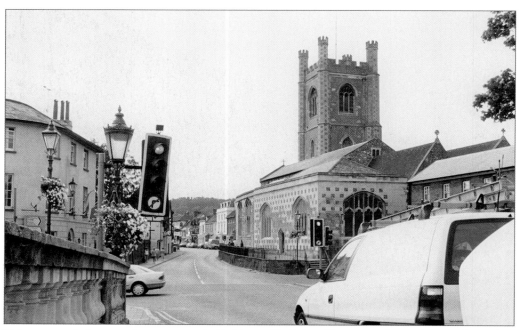

This crossroads is now a busy one controlled by traffic lights. The tree in front of the Red Lion has gone but otherwise the scene is little changed.

Towards the bridge from Hart Street, *c.* 1900. The timber-framed houses with tall gables date from the sixteenth century, and the nearest of them is reputed to be the birthplace of William Lenthall, the famous Speaker of the House of Commons who refused to admit Charles I in 1642. The houses have been converted to commercial premises, including a haircutting and shampooing salon. (*Bushells Photographic*)

The gabled houses have been well restored as offices, but the Georgian building nearest to the camera has acquired some bogus timbering and is now a café. In the distance can be seen the new Royal Regatta Headquarters on the other side of the river (see p. 50).

The delightful Chantry House is probably the oldest timber-framed building in Henley and stands between St Mary's churchyard and the Red Lion Hotel. Because of the slope of the land, the three-storey building has a two-storey façade on the churchyard side. A recent survey has suggested that it was built as a merchant's house in the early sixteenth century with storerooms on the ground floor, a shop on the first floor and living quarters above. In the early seventeenth century it was used as schoolrooms by the free Grammar School and Lady Periam's School. It is seen here in the 1890s after it had been sold to the Red Lion. (*Bushells Photographic*)

The Chantry House was restored in the 1920s as a memorial to the Rev. Canon John Frederic Maul (rector of Henley since 1883), and presented to the church. There is now renewed concern about decay and death-watch beetle in its timbers.

This lithograph view of Hart Street looking from St Mary's Church towards the old Town Hall was published in 1859. On the extreme right is Longlands, a particularly handsome house with a pedimented doorway which dates from about 1720 and was then one of the most fashionable residences in the town. (*Bushells Photographic*)

The same view today shows how the ironwork railings around the church have been much reduced, making the approach to the church much more open. The buildings opposite Longlands look very different with their mock Tudor façades.

This baker's and confectioner's shop at 16 Hart Street has a window display very typical of its era, *c.* 1910. It was for some years run by George Jay, and in 1911 became Hughes Bros dairy. (*Henley Standard*)

Although the building has been painted white and the merchandise on display is very different, the old shopfront is almost unchanged.

Hart Street packed with people attending an agricultural fair and sale, *c.* 1900. This was an annual event, and horses for sale were trotted up and down for viewing. Attention is focused on the premises of Simmons and Sons, auctioneers, valuers and land agents, but it appears that the bidding has not yet begun. (*Bushells Photographic*)

No. 18 Hart Street was an antiques shop for many years but is now again an estate agent's office under the name of F.P.D. Savills, International Property Consultants. Simmons has since split into two separate businesses, Simmons and Sons and Simmons and Lawrence, both of which trade in Bell Street.

Looking up Hart Street towards the Market Place and Town Hall from St Mary's tower, *c.* 1930. Motorised traffic has made its appearance in Henley but the policeman at the crossroads with Duke Street and Bell Street does not appear to be too overworked! (*Bushells Photographic*)

Henley has not changed a great deal from this viewpoint except for the traffic, but the urban area has spread on to the distant hillside, once the preserve of grand houses such as Westfield House with their extensive grounds (see p. 124).

Looking towards the Town Hall, *c.* 1880. The grand obelisk in the foreground was put up as a milestone in the 1780s at the crossroads of Hart Street and Bell Street, and three of its sides were inscribed with the distances to Reading, Oxford and London. (*Bushells Photographic*)

The same view today shows a pedestrianised Market Place and the new Town Hall, which was completed in 1901.

In 1885 the obelisk was moved to Northfield End as a signpost and was replaced in the Market Place by an elaborate drinking fountain in porphyry and stone with a crocketed spire, erected to the memory of Greville Phillimore. He was rector of Henley from 1867 to 1883 and he earned the gratitude of the town for his numerous benefactions. The four iron lamps were removed not long after this photograph was taken, *c.* 1885. (*Bushells Photographic*)

In 1903 the fountain was removed to its present location outside the west door of St Mary's Church.

Hart Street from the Market Place, 1960s. Motorists were faced with a confusing array of directional signs at the junction, and not long after this picture was taken a standard system of signs was introduced in which capital letters were replaced by initial capitals followed by lower-case letters, making them easier to read. The large Tudor-style building which appears rather out of scale with the rest of the street was built as the London and County Bank in 1892. (*Bushells Photographic*)

The directional signs are now positioned on the approaches to the junction rather than actually on it, and Hart Street has lost its strip of garden down the centre. The bank is now trading as Barclay's.

The Three Tuns public house and Gabriel Machin's butcher's shop in the Market Place, 1950s. Machin has been in business in the Market Place as a poulterer and pork butcher since the 1880s and the family also ran a grocer's shop in Northfield End. (*W.H. Brakspear and Co. Ltd*)

The pub and Machin's shop are still in business today. The butcher's shop is now owned by the Marett family, though still trading under the name of Machin, and it has competed successfully with the supermarkets by specialising in unusual and high-quality meats and fish.

Processions in Hart Street to celebrate the coronation of King Edward VII in August 1902. A sedan chair mounted on a bicycle follows Henley Volunteer Fire Brigade's elaborate float, and behind it there is a large group carrying a banner, 'From our river'. (*Bushells Photographic*)

The old Town Hall and Market Place in a print of 1855. Alderman Bradshaw demolished the Market House Guildhall and Gaol in 1795 and replaced them by this Town Hall which he designed himself, giving it a classical façade and an open ground floor for use as a corn market. Office accommodation was later extended by enclosing the ground floor. (*Bushells Photographic*)

Bunting is strung across the street in place of the flags in this view of Hart Street, but queuing traffic now dominates the scene.

A busy day in Hart Street in the early twentieth century, with the new Town Hall in the distance. The old Town Hall was taken down in 1898 and re-erected on Crazies Hill as a private house. Its replacement, completed in 1901, satisfied the Corporation's need for extra office accommodation and was designed by Henry T. Hare.

A similar scene today, showing the flowerbeds and pollarded trees that now occupy the centre of the Market Place.

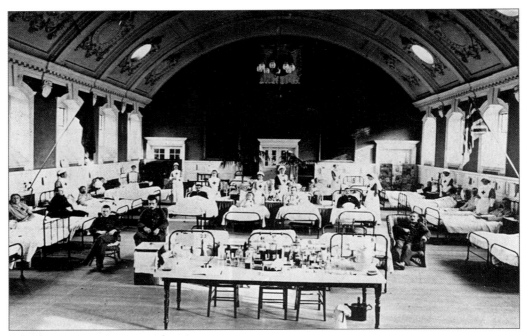

The Town Hall being used as a military hospital during the First World War. Twenty-four beds were laid out on the upper floor in August 1914 and the first patients arrived in October to be nursed by the Henley Voluntary Aid Detachment. (*River and Rowing Museum, Henley-on-Thames*)

The upper room of the Town Hall is currently being repaired and refurbished.

CHAPTER TWO

READING ROAD/DUKE STREET TO BELL STREET & NORTHFIELD END

Harpsden Road, off Reading Road, under a blanket of snow, *c.* 1900. Henley was growing rapidly by the end of the nineteenth century. To meet the need for accommodation for those working in the expanding service industries such as the railway, hotels and shops, Harpsden Road and several adjacent terraces were laid out by developer William Hamilton in the 1890s.

The appearance of Harpsden Road has changed little, except that most households now have at least one car which has to be parked on the roadside.

Upton Lodge, on Reading Road, *c.* 1900. The boom in building brought not only terraced houses but also large elegant villas close to the town centre. The middle classes were prospering following the arrival of the railway and many were attracted to the town by its pleasant situation and its reputation as the home of the Regatta.

The house has since been demolished and the site is now occupied by houses in Upton Close.

The Congregational church and Caxton House at the junction of Reading Road and Station Road, *c.* 1910. Thomas Higgs moved his printing business from Bell Street to Caxton House in 1885, where he became official printer to the Royal Regatta and published the *Henley Free Press*. In 1900 the business was bought by Charles Luker, and he ran Higgs and Co. and the renamed *Henley Standard* for many years, during which time he served as Mayor of Henley on eight occasions. He was awarded an OBE in 1954 and died in 1968 aged ninety-one. (*River and Rowing Museum, Henley-on-Thames*)

The *Henley Standard* remains a thriving local newspaper. It is still part of the Higgs Group and the current chairman is John Luker, Charles' grandson. Their offices have been completely refurbished and now look out on to a busy mini-roundabout where the railings once stood.

A view of Duke Street looking towards the crossroads with Hart Street, 1860s. The street was narrow and inconvenient, and soon became muddy in wet weather.

The appearance of the street was changed radically in about 1870 when the west side was demolished by the Henley Local Government Board to widen access for traffic. All the left-hand side has been rebuilt since then and some of the right-hand too.

Street entertainment outside Stanley Mead's hairdresser's at 29 Duke Street, *c.* 1890. The cart carries the message 'The Fireman's Wedding and other recitations by the monkey', and the doorway to the right is marked in chalk over the lintel as 'The monkey's home, organs to let'. (*Henley Standard*) *Inset*: The 'monkey's home' has long gone and 29 Duke Street is now occupied by Thaine's electrical shop.

The Wesleyan chapel in Duke Street was erected in 1874 but it was closed in 1980 as maintenance costs escalated. Here it is seen during demolition in 1983. (*South Oxfordshire District Council*)

The site in Duke Street is now occupied by the Henley Piano Galleries.

Queen Mary visiting the premises of John Hawkins, fine china and glass dealer, at 7 to 11 Duke Street, in the 1920s. Queen Mary was an avid collector of tableware and antiques, and she visited this shop on several occasions. The business continued in Duke Street until 1950. (*Bushells Photographic*)

No. 11 Duke Street is now occupied by the Imperial Cancer Research Fund's charity shop.

Looking into Bell Street, with the Market Place to the left and Hart Street to the right, *c.* 1900. At the crossroads stands the drinking fountain erected to the memory of Greville Phillimore (see p. 20) and behind it can be seen the premises of Monk and Sons, a draper's store founded by Charles Monk before 1883. On the other corner is S.H. Higgins, bookseller and newsagent, which before the First World War became Timothy White, Cash Chemists (see Frontispiece).

Monk and Sons closed in the 1950s and the site is now occupied by Bonus Print and Boots the Chemist. The building on the opposite side of the road has been reduced in height but is once again a stationer's, trading under the name of Martins and incorporating a post office.

This view of Bell Street in the 1890s shows a delightful variety of shops. In the foreground, the Halfway House was run by publican W. Bunce and seems to sell everything from ales and porter to fruit, vegetables and even rabbits! Beyond it can be seen a tobacconist, a fruiterer and William Simpkins' drapery and haberdashery store with its large shop windows. (*Bushells Photographic*)

Woolworths now occupies the site of the Halfway House, and Clintons cards and Clarks occupy the much-altered premises of Simpkins. The bollards in the foreground have been introduced as part of a traffic-calming scheme to make the street almost as pedestrian-friendly as it was in 1890!

Bell Street on a fine summers day in 1895, this time taken from in front of Simpkins store and looking towards the other side of the street. On the far right is the Duke of Cumberland public house. Records of the pub go back to the 1760s; it was named in honour of the Duke of Cumberland who defeated the Jacobites at the Battle of Culloden in 1746.

Clarks shoe shop has replaced Simpkins and the pub has acquired some mock timber-framing, being renamed Ye Olde Bell in 1920, but the buildings have not changed much. It is interesting, however, to contrast the styles of summer clothing seen in these two pictures.

Henley's Picture Palace cinema at 33 Bell Street, 1920s. The cinema was opened as early as 1911 in premises which had been a roller-skating rink. (*Bushells Photographic*)

In 1937 the Picture Palace was pulled down to make way for the Regal. This in turn was demolished in 1993 as part of the Waitrose development, and the new store was opened at the end of the following year. The development had been six years in the planning, during which a vigorous Save the Regal campaign had been fought, with high profile appeals and calls for a public planning enquiry. A new Regal multiscreen cinema was opened on a different site in 1997.

The Regal cinema. (*Newsquest (Oxfordshire)*)

Bell Street looking north, *c*. 1895. On the left can be seen Alfred Pither's butcher's shop, famous for its home-cured hams and the 'celebrated Henley sausages', and beyond it are Henry Crocker's shoe shop and the Bull Inn with its projecting lamp.

Much of the left-hand side of the street was demolished in the 1960s and rebuilt as part of the Waitrose development, but the Bull Inn survives. On the other side the changes are limited mainly to the shopfronts. Burton Dining Rooms has long gone and looks very different as an interior design shop.

Northfield End, *c.* 1905. The broad space to either side of the road as it merges from Bell Street into Northfield End encouraged the building of some fine houses in the eighteenth and early nineteenth centuries, including many with attractive diaper brickwork in different colours and elaborate classical door surrounds.

Northfield End had retained its appeal despite the cluttered appearance that parked cars can create. Many of the grandest houses are now occupied by prestige offices.

Looking towards Northfield End from the Oxford Road, 1892. The obelisk was moved to the fork of the Marlow and Oxford Roads from the town centre in 1885 and converted for use as a signpost.

In 1970 the obelisk was moved again, this time to Mill Meadows. A mini-roundabout has replaced it on the Oxford Road.

CHAPTER THREE

THE BRIDGE & RIVER

Relaxing on Henley bridge on a summer's afternoon, *c.* 1900. The bridge was rebuilt in 1786 to designs by William Hayward, and he gave it elegant lines and particularly fine detailing in the stonework, including the balustraded parapet and carved heads of Thames and Isis over the central arches. On the Berkshire side of the river can be seen the Carpenter's Arms facing the road and boathouses along the riverside.

The bridge itself has changed little over the last century apart from the modern lighting. However the Carpenter's Arms and boathouses have been replaced by the new Henley Royal Regatta Headquarters, which was completed in 1984 in a bold contemporary style.

An animated view towards the bridge, taken from a print of about 1830. At this time the river was the town's lifeblood and was heavily used by sailing barges carrying goods from London and beyond. On the bank on the left, where Thameside now stands, could be found wharves and warehouses. The tall building just before the bridge is the Angel Inn. (*Bushells Photographic*)

Looking from the bridge towards Remenham, *c.* 1910. On the extreme right is the Carpenter's Arms, whose origins can be traced back to 1714, and the white building further down on the other side of the road is the Little Angel. (*Bushells Photographic*)

The Carpenter's Arms was demolished in 1984 to make way for the Henley Royal Regatta Headquarters, part of which can be seen on the right. Remenham appears much more wooded than it was a hundred years ago, and it is certainly no longer safe to loiter in the road!

The entrance to Henley Bridge on the Berkshire side was barred by a toll-gate until 1873, by which time the builders had recouped the original £10,000 cost of the bridge's construction. In this photograph of about 1900 the progress of the carts towards Henley is unimpeded, and the leisurely pace of the traffic means that keeping to the left is not essential!

Roadmarkings dominate the view today but little else has changed except for the demolition of Toll Gate Cottage on the right in the 1960s. The side road in the foreground leads down to the Leander Club (see p. 60) and the riverside meadows. This junction becomes a bottleneck in Regatta week.

Thameside looking towards the bridge, *c.* 1900. Because it was near the railway station, this was a favourite place for day trippers to hire a boat.

Looking up Thameside today, with the church tower behind and the white painted Angel in the distance and on the right. The booth next to the slipway in the foreground, now used by Alf Parrott Moorings Ltd, used to be the ticket office for J. Arlett and Sons who hired out motor launches.

The timber-framed Old Granary, which faced the river on the corner of Thameside and Friday Street. It was probably built in the fifteenth or sixteenth century as a warehouse for the port at a time when Henley owed much of its prosperity to the river trade with London. By 1900, when this picture was taken, the trade had all but collapsed: the building appears to be in use for general storage and to be in a poor state of repair. (*Bushells Photographic*)

The Old Granary has been converted into very desirable residences and much of the old timberwork has been preserved.

In this photograph of about 1887 Friday Street presents a scene of picturesque dilapidation! This was the industrial end of town, and Grey's Brewery, an ironworks and a printing works could be found in the near vicinity. Many of the houses were overcrowded slums divided by narrow alleyways.

Much of Friday Street was condemned for demolition in the 1930s but was saved by the outbreak of war in 1939. The houses have since been restored and converted into attractive dwellings. The Anchor Inn, on the extreme left, is still in business, though no doubt serving a very different clientele.

Looking towards the bridge and Red Lion Hotel, 1880s. To the right of the hotel can be seen the arched entrance to large hotel stable blocks which stretch along the riverside. Steam launches like the one moored to the quay and the one pulling away became very fashionable towards the end of the Victorian era.

The wisteria on the Red Lion Hotel appears less rampant in this photograph, and the adjacent stable block has been converted into hotel accommodation and conference rooms. To the right, the white-painted Century Galleries occupies the Red Lion boathouse, which was built in 1889 to replace some of the stables seen in the top photograph. Behind stands the tower of St Mary's Church.

Riverside from the bridge, 1920s. The arched entrance to the Red Lion Hotel stable block can be seen on the left with a charming riverside lawn in front of it, and beyond are the Red Lion boathouses. The lawn was a favoured place to watch the Regatta, and originally the race course started at Temple Island and finished here. Less seemly were the brawls that sometimes took place between the boatmen on Riverside; half a dozen boat hire firms operated between the bridge and Wharfe Lane and the rivalry between them was often anything but friendly!

Sadly the Red Lion lawn was lost to road widening when the one-way system was introduced, and only a small paved area survives.

Riverside at the bottom of New Street, 1892. The boathouses on the right belonged to boatbuilders H.E. Hobbs and Sons, and the gabled building to the left of the white cottages served as stables for Brakspear's Brewery and was later used by the Henley Rowing Club.

Hobbs' boathouses have been converted into luxury riverside residences with their own private moorings.

Before the river was brought under control in the twentieth century, Henley used to suffer from frequent flooding, and the severity of the 'Great Flood' of 1894 can be judged from this view from New Street towards the river. The picture also shows some of Henley's most elegant early eighteenth-century houses built in the local brick with heavy wooden cornices, and on the right one of the town's gas lights is nicely silhouetted. (*Bushells Photographic*)

Cars now park on the riverside which was so deeply under water in 1894. The houses on the left have not changed their outward appearances, except for the door canopies which have been replaced in different styles.

The Leander Club of London provided an umpire for the first Henley Regatta in 1839 and was soon competing regularly in the event. This photograph shows Leicester House in Northfield End flying the Leander flag in about 1902, probably because a Leander crew was staying there for the duration of Regatta week.

In 1897 the Leander Club built itself a permanent riverside home in Henley and is presently engaged in a thorough refurbishment of the buildings. Founded in 1818, it is Britain's oldest surviving rowing club and its membership is made up of distinguished rowers and those who have served the world of international rowing. This view of the club headquarters today is taken from the river.

CHAPTER FOUR

AT SCHOOL & AT WORK

The British School on Reading Road, 1904. The school was built next to the Congregational church in 1856, and a traditional brick and flint construction was chosen for its construction. British Schools were established by a voluntary organisation, the British and Foreign Schools Society, with the aim of building an 'honest, God-fearing, Church-going population'. They were unsectarian.

The school closed in 1932 and the building was destroyed by fire in the 1960s, except for the far left wing which is now occupied by a carpet business.

Pupils at the National School, Gravel Hill, 1904. This schoolroom for girls, built in 1879, was part of the Church of England school established in St Mary's Hall in New Street in 1817. Unlike the British Schools, the National Schools insisted on denominational teaching.

The school buildings now house the Henley College Drama School, but the character of the building has been preserved.

The classroom of the Church of England Infants' School off Gravel Hill, photographed in 1906. The classes must have been large and the classroom appears rather comfortless, heated by a single stove in winter.

This room is also used by Henley College, this time as an administrative office.

Pupils ready to begin lessons at Trinity Voluntary School in Greys Hill, 1906. Voluntary schools originally catered for the children of poorer people, who, with the exception of those who won scholarships to a grammar school, were denied a secondary school education.

The old school has been converted into a private house and this picture shows a class in progress at the school's present premises in Vicarage Road. It is interesting to contrast the formal layout of the old schoolroom with the more open-plan classroom of today, its walls displaying work produced by the children.

A rare and very early photograph of Henley's first postman, probably taken in about 1860. As well as his leather bags for carrying letters, he is equipped with a bugle and a walking stick. (*Bushells Photographic*)

Today's postmen dress very differently.

The Super and his cat! An unnamed superintendent in the Henley Police models the latest uniform in about 1900, with his pet cat perched precariously on his cap. One can only speculate on the background to this picture!

A sergeant from the Thames Valley Police Force kindly poses for the camera in the latest uniform, but declines to sport any animals, friendly or otherwise, on his cap!

Henley Volunteer Fire Brigade, *c.* 1890. The Brigade was established in 1868 and was for many years stationed in the Market Place near to the Town Hall. At the time of this picture its strength amounted to fourteen firemen, a foreman, a superintendent engineer, a horse-drawn steam engine (in the picture), a manual engine and a hose reel. (*Bushells Photographic*)

Henley's retained fire station now has two fire engines in its West Street station and is part of Oxfordshire County Council's Fire Service. It is interesting to note how the old uniforms have been replaced by high technology protective clothing.

Stuart Turner works, *c.* 1920. The firm was established in 1906 to build parts for engines, but it soon turned to manufacturing motor-cycles and moved to its current premises at 43 Market Place in 1917. Thriving on War Office contracts to supply small air-cooled petrol engines, the firm expanded into marine engines, electric motors and pumps. (*River and Rowing Museum, Henley-on-Thames*)

Stuart Turner Ltd is now a world leader in the manufacture of pumps and employs over 100 people. In December 1999 the firm moved into large new premises on the site of its old workshops behind the Market Place façade. This photograph is of the interior of their shop.

The employees of Benjamin Reeves, corn dealer, pictured outside one of their premises in Bell Street in 1900. The four men, G. Wooten, J. Airey, F. Ames and J. Webb, are wearing typical working clothes of the period including waistcoats and cloth caps.

This building in Bell Street, one of Reeves' addresses, is now occupied by a retail unit which was vacant when this picture was taken.

Hales and Son's Model Steam Bakery was founded at 20 Market Place by Stephen Hales and, according to an advertisement in 1906, sold 'Pure household bread, brown bread, Hovis bread, milk bread, Veda bread and Vienna bread'. This photograph was taken in about 1893. (*Bushells Photographic*)

A corresponding scene, from the Patisserie Franco-Belge, shows more stainless steel equipment, but the skills required are no doubt much the same.

Mr Turton Green behind the counter of his chemist's shop in Bell Street, *c.* 1900. The serried ranks of dark bottles seem to lend an air of fear and mystique to his profession.

The sales area of Moss the Chemist in modern Bell Street gives an altogether more welcoming impression.

G.T. Savage's delivery cart, seen here taking part in a horse parade in 1900. George Savage ran a cabinet-making and upholstery business at 37 Bell Street.

The Bell Street Motor Works, 1930. This garage served the motorists of Henley for many years from their town centre premises, and at the time this picture was taken it was being run by Mr R.H. Cain. (*Bushells Photographic*)

The new Bell Court development of town houses has replaced a large part of this side of Bell Street. Many local people voiced their wish that residential development would be preferable to commercial use in such a prime location.

H.E. Hobbs and Sons' premises in Station Road, 1901. Hobbs was established in 1870 and its boat hire business prospered as Henley became a popular destination for holidays and day-trips, easily accessible by train from Reading and beyond. By the end of the century it had acquired extensive premises in Station Road and on Riverside, and was described in the trade directories as 'builders and hirers of boats and steam and electric launches.'

Hobbs and Sons Ltd still hire boats in the summer months, and the premises on Station Road now operate as Hobbs Marine Store Ltd.

The yard at Brakspear's brewery, New Street, with a horse-drawn dray about to depart, *c.* 1900. Henley was once renowned for its malthouses and breweries but now only W.H. Brakspear and Sons survives. Robert Brakspear founded the company in 1779 when he opened his brewery in Bell Street, and in 1812 his son William moved to these premises in New Street. The New Street brewery had been built by Benjamin Sarney in the early eighteenth century, and soon afterwards the family bought the house and malt kiln to the west which now serve as Brakspear's offices. The property was finally bought from Sarney's descendants by W.H. Brakspear and Sons in 1856. (*River and Rowing Museum, Henley-on-Thames*)

Brakspear's yard has not changed a great deal. The building on the far right is now a shop selling Brakspear's products, souvenirs and other wines and spirits.

Soon after the takeover of the rival Greys Brewery, Brakespear's built these huge malthouses in New Street in 1899 and closed their other malthouses in the town. They are seen here in 1978. (*South Oxfordshire District Council*)

Malting ceased in 1972 and the buildings are now occupied as offices by AIT Group plc, computer software consultants. The outward appearance of the building has been conserved as far as possible, even to the extent of replacing the original ventilation cowls on the roof with replicas in fibreglass.

The bottling plant at Brakspear's brewery, *c.* 1900. It all looks very labour intensive. (*River and Rowing Museum, Henley-on-Thames*)

Filling metal casks in the brewery today. The process is much more mechanised and appears more hygenic.

The blacksmith's forge at Brakspear's brewery is seen in action, *c.* 1900. At a time when beer was transported in metal hooped barrels on metal-tyred drays pulled by iron-shod horses, the skills of the cooper and blacksmith were in great demand.

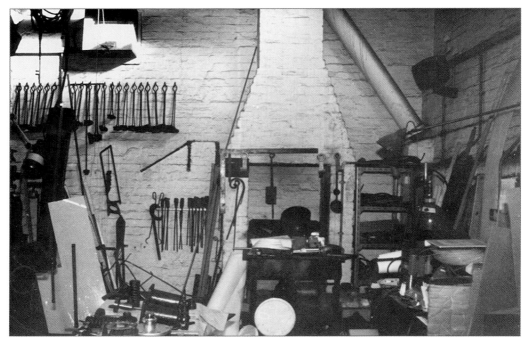

The forge today is used for general storage and the blacksmith's fire has been long cold, but many of the original tools have been left undisturbed. One wonders for how long?

CHAPTER FIVE

TRANSPORT
THEN & NOW

Seeing the town and its surroundings from the river has always been one of Henley's main attractions, and visitors have taken to the water in an infinite variety of boats. By the end of the nineteenth century steam launches had become very popular and this fine launch, the *Conway*, is taking a group of guests on an outing from Park Place in 1898.

Sadly the steam launches have disappeared from the river but the wide variety of boats seems undiminished, some of them well equipped for the open seas.

Henley's prosperity suffered when the Great Western Railway was built through Reading and Twyford thus bypassing the town, but a link with the main line at Twyford was finally established in 1857. This photograph shows the station in about 1910, with cabs waiting under the canopy for passengers. (© *Crown Copyright NMR*)

The original station was demolished in 1975 except for the platform canopies. Nine years later the present station was built as part of a joint development with Hallmark Cards, which entailed shortening the line and building the new station further from Station Road. Plans have been mooted to rebuild the station again on a new site further from the town centre, but they have met with considerable local opposition.

Looking towards the station from the platforms, 1919. The structure on the right was a water tower to supply the steam engines, and beyond was a turntable. Although at the end of the line, Henley was a busy station and by the early twentieth century, when the fastest journey time to Paddington had been reduced to fifty minutes, nearly 100,000 tickets a year were being sold. A return second-class ticket to London then cost 6s 6d. (*National Railway Museum, York*)

The large car park on the left has been laid out on the site of the former goods yard, which became redundant when goods traffic ceased in 1964. The white-painted platform canopy dates from 1904 and is the only part of the old station to survive. Behind it can be seen the station offices and the high roof of the Hallmark Cards building, which stands where the old station used to be.

The growing popularity of the Royal Regatta in the Edwardian era owed much to easy access to the town by railway, and extra trains from Paddington, Didcot and Oxford were laid on. In 1898 over 37,000 passengers were carried over the three days. The station was always decorated for the occasion, as shown in this photograph of 1952.

Thames Trains have proudly signed Henley as 'Home of the Royal Regatta', but not as many visitors come to the Regatta by train as they used to.

The Station House block of shops and offices and Henley railway station, from Station Road, *c.* 1980. (*Henley Standard*)

The Hallmark Cards development replaced Station House and the site of much of the old railway station in 1984. The new station can be found to the right of the office block.

Henley station from the booking hall, showing its British Railways signing, 1961. The smoke troughs and chimneys suspended from the roof were introduced in 1904 to take the smoke from standing steam locomotives. (© *Crown Copyright NMR*)

The view today on to the sole surviving platform.

A British Railways locomotive preparing to depart from Henley station in October 1955, just three years before steam-hauled branch services were withdrawn and replaced by new diesel railcars. (*National Railway Museum, York*)

The service today is operated by Thames Trains Sprinters like this one. Most passengers for London Paddington have to change at Twyford or Reading, but there is an early morning direct train, the Regatta Express.

The Busy Bee, Brakspear's Foden steam dray, leaving the Little Angel in Remenham, *c.* 1910. The wagon's name is an allusion to the firm's emblem of a bee. Steam power must have made deliveries much easier in the hilly country around Henley.

Brakspear's fleet of modern drays may be more efficient but it looks much less picturesque!

A group about to set off in a charabanc, *c.* 1920. Many employers organised annual outings by charabanc for their workers, often to the seaside, but this vehicle does not look very comfortable for

a long journey. (*Bushells Photographic*) *Inset*: Thames Travel's buses, which connect Henley with Wallingford and Oxford, offer a much more comfortable ride!

An early Daimler removal lorry of about 1920. George Girdler started as a carrier but his business interests soon expanded into furniture removals and operating a bus service to Twyford and Wargrave. He recognised before most businesses the advantages of the new telephone service, and his number was Henley 275. (*Bushells Photographic*)

Girdler's business was run from this house at 115 Reading Road.

CHAPTER SIX

INNS & HOTELS

Enjoying the summer sun on the river terrace of the Angel Inn, *c.* 1910. The Angel has been welcoming locals and visitors alike since the eighteenth century, and its picturesque bay windows, irregular rooflines and superb position by the bridge make it a familiar landmark of the town. Some of the guests here are arriving by punt.

The Angel remains as popular today and has been smartened with a wash of white paint.

The Hart Street façade of the Angel, photographed in 1904 during a walking race from Twyford railway bridge to Henley Town Hall, a distance of just over 5 miles. The leading walker is Ernest John Clegg, who completed the distance in fifty-eight minutes and forty-five seconds.

The junction at the entrance to the bridge is now a busy one, but the Angel has changed little on the outside other than the new signing.

The prime site on the other side of the bridge to the Angel is occupied by the Red Lion, one of Henley's mos
prestigious hotels and one with a long history as a coaching inn. Its origins are said to date from the sixteent
century and King Charles I stayed here on his way to Oxford in 1632. The present building dates from th
eighteenth century when it was rebuilt to accommodate travellers arriving on the turnpike road from London
Here we see it during the war years in August 1942.

Apart from the cutting back of the wisteria from the entrance porch, this side of the hotel has changed little. Th
same, however, cannot be said of the traffic!

The vestibule and hall of the Red Lion Hotel are furnished very much in the taste of the period in this photograph of 1897. Foliage is very much in evidence, including a particularly exuberant display of palms in the hall, which is lit by a domed skylight.

Recent refurbishments have stripped the woodwork, carpeted the floor, removed the stained glass – and dealt a fatal blow to the potted palms!

The old Royal Hotel on the corner of Station Road and Thameside. It was built as a private house by local entrepreneur Robert Outhwaite in 1864, but by 1872 he had converted it into an hotel. Many of the rooms had views towards Marsh Meadows and lock, and the 14 acres of grounds surrounding the hotel featured a croquet lawn and a terrace walk in the Italian style.

The hotel was not a commercial success and in 1899–1900 most of it was demolished and a second Royal Hotel built in its place. It too closed in about 1925 and the block was converted into flats. This view is of the river frontage of the block, now known as Royal Mansions and River Terrace.

The Packhorse public house at 19 Northfield End, 1950s. The Packhorse had a long history and a Richard Powny is recorded as publican, and probably owner, from 1774 to 1780. By 1826 it was certainly in the ownership of Brakspear's brewery and in the 1850s it was the starting point for James Farley's carrier services to High Wycombe and to Reading and Twyford. (*W.H. Brakspear and Co. Ltd*)

The Packhorse closed in 1964 and the building was empty when this photograph was taken.

Christmas farmers' market in the yard of the White Hart Hotel, Hart Street, 1927. The White Hart was the oldest pub in Henley and its origins go back at least to 1466. In the 1830s it was the main coaching inn in the town with stabling for seventy-three horses, and after the collapse of the coaching trade the hotel used its large stable yard for weekly farmers' markets. (*Bushells Photographic*)

The White Hart closed in 1996 and in 1999 it was completely refurbished as the ASK pizza and pasta restaurant. This view shows the old inn yard, and through the archway in the back range can be seen the second yard beyond, where the markets used to be held.

The Bull Inn in Bell Street, 1974. This fine timber-framed inn probably dates from the fifteenth century with bay windows added in the mid-seventeenth. It was also once a busy coaching inn, but by the 1850s the coach services had ceased and the Bull was patronised mainly by farmers coming into town for the markets. (*South Oxfordshire District Council*)

The Bull Inn remains a popular Brakspear's public house, and, like many others, has turned to serving food as well as drinks.

Henley's growing self-confidence in the late Victorian era is superbly expressed in the Imperial Hotel, built in 1897 in a flamboyant Jacobean style. The hotel, seen here in the 1920s, was built near the railway station to greet fashionable guests as they arrived by train. (*Bushells Photographic*)

The Imperial has been faithfully restored to its former glory in recent years and its paintwork now looks smarter than ever.

The Rivermead Private Hotel was one of the numerous small hotels and bed and breakfast establishments built to accommodate the increasing numbers of visitors brought to the town by the railway. Seen here in about 1925, it had a pleasant garden and was conveniently situated near to the station with access to the towing path and river.

The hotel has since been converted into private residences.

The Three Horseshoes public house next to the Congregational church in Reading Road, *c.* 1900. The building was demolished for road widening in 1930 and the name was transferred to premises in Harpsden Road (see p. 106). (*Bushells Photographic*)

The site on Reading Road is now occupied by a stone-mason's and funeral director's business, set well back from the busy road.

The 'new' Three Horseshoes public house was opened by Brakspear's on the junction of Harpsden Road and Reading Road in 1930, when the old premises on Reading Road were demolished. This picture was taken in 1986.

The junction today has lost its telephone kiosk but otherwise appears little changed.

The Basketmaker's Arms at the top of Gravel Hill, 1950s. At this time there were thirty-seven public houses in the town, but many of them were so small that they were insufficient to provide a living and the landlord had to find other employment during the day. The Basketmaker's Arms is first recorded as a beerhouse and lodging house in 1841. (*W.H. Brakspear and Co. Ltd*)

The pub closed in 1972, and is now a private house called the Old Basketmaker's Arms.

The Travellers Rest
public house during
rebuilding, 1900.
This popular pub stood
at the top of the Fair Mile
where the roads to
Oxford and Watlington
fork, and here we see the
new premises being built
behind the original
building, which was
subsequently demolished.
Inset: The later building
was in its turn taken
down for road widening
in the 1930s, and
nothing remains of the
Travellers Rest today.

The Oddfellows Arms in Church Street, 1950s. It was certainly in existence in the 1860s when it was bought by Brakspear's brewery, but it may date back to the 1840s. (*W.H. Brakspear and Co. Ltd*)

The pub closed in 1985 after the retirement of popular landlady Mrs Lillian Skillings. She had been the licensee for twenty-two years, running the business single-handed for twenty-one years after the death of her husband. After closure it was delicensed by Brakspear's, and it is now a private house.

CHAPTER SEVEN

THE REGATTA

Spectators arriving on Thameside from the railway station are being approached by a man in a white coat offering boats and canoes for hire. This picture, taken in about 1890, captures some of the excitement of the day.

Today few visitors arrive by train and the congestion is to be found on the town's approach roads instead. The Carpenter's Arms by the bridge on the other side of the river has been replaced by the Henley Royal Regatta Headquarters.

Congestion on the river, 1890s. Many spectators liked to get into the spirit of the occasion by taking to the water themselves in every conceivable type of craft, whether rowed, punted or steam-powered. It must have been difficult keeping the course clear for the races.

Many people today also like to bring their boats to Henley during Regatta week, but at least they are made to park them away from the race courses.

Spectators, boats and tents on Lion Meadow, 1902. Crowds pack the riverbank and the press enclosure can be seen in the middle distance.

A similar scene today as spectators watch the proceedings or make for the refreshment tents.

During Regatta week the banks of the river used to be lined with luxuriously furnished houseboats, and owners vied with each other in the lavishness of their accommodation and hospitality. The houseboats were towed to their moorings by a steamer, and in 1888 more than eighty applications for moorings were made to the Thames Conservators. This view of the riverside taken in 1896 shows the *Maid of Kent* and *River Holme Barge*.

The houseboats are no more but the Oxford College Barge has been beautifully restored in recent years.

Houseboat parties were famous for their hospitality and became firmly established in the English calendar of fashionable events. This group is on board the houseboat *Stella* in the 1890s.

Members of the Cretans Society recreating the elegance of the past on board the Oxford College Barge, 1999. The restoration of the barge in recent years has been a major achievement.

Relaxing after the race under the shade of a tree, 1890s. The numerous tents erected on the meadows provided further places for cool relaxation.

The meadows today are largely filled with parked cars. However, a well-chosen spot under a leafy tree can be an excellent place to share a picnic and a bottle of Pimms.

Fashionable guests viewing the races from a houseboat, 1898. It is interesting to observe the variety of hats being worn in this gathering.

Stands have replaced the houseboats as the places to see and be seen, and hats have not gone entirely out of fashion. The Regatta has retained its place in the social calendar, but business hospitality now accounts for many of the visitors. Election to the Stewards' Enclosure, however, remains a coveted honour, and care is taken to ensure that accomplished oarsmen are still well represented.

Viewing the races from the Enclosures, 1902.

Ninety-seven years later, and the scene appears little changed.

King George V and Queen Mary visiting the Regatta, 1912. This first grandstand was a temporary structure, but the following year a permanent one was constructed in front of Phyllis Court.

The grandstand built in 1913 was replaced by this stand in 1993. It retains the character of its predecessor but has the advantage of heating and double-glazed windows so it can be used throughout the year.

CHAPTER EIGHT

OUT OF TOWN

The Fair Mile looking north-west, *c.* 1893. The fine avenues of elm trees were planted by Sir Thomas Stapleton, Lord of the Manor of Benson, in 1751, but sadly they had to be felled in 1953 and have since been replanted with oaks and limes. The shallow roadside ditch used to fill with water from the Assenden spring in wet weather.

The Fair Mile remains one of Henley's great assets, and on the whole modern development has not been allowed to encroach on it.

The disused Smith Hospital in the Fair Mile, 1980s. Originally built as an isolation hospital in 1892, it turned to caring for autistic children in the 1950s and was closed by West Berkshire Health Authority in July 1988 because of high running costs. (*Henley Standard*)

The hospital buildings have been demolished and Henley software company AIT moved into new offices built on the site in 1999. AIT, which started in a tiny office in Bell Street, is now a market leader in supplying computer software to the financial services industry.

Westfield House in 1926. Westfield is typical of the several large houses in extensive grounds which were put up in the late nineteenth and early twentieth centuries for Henley's prospering middle classes. It had a splendid location overlooking the town from above Gravel Hill.

The house has been demolished and the site is now occupied by modern housing.

Marsh Mills House was once the home of the mill owner and his family. This picture was taken in 1901 for an auction catalogue and it shows the extensive gardens.

The house has since undergone substantial refurbishment, and the garden has also been redesigned after the removal of the waterside embankment and railings.

Marsh Lock keeper's cottage. The old photograph was taken before the cottage underwent major restoration in the 1870s.

The keeper's cottage is seen here thoroughly restored; the lock itself was reconstructed in 1998 and now has electrically driven gates. Although commercial traffic on the river has now virtually ceased, the locks are now busier than ever in the summer months as boating holidays become more popular.

View from Marsh Lock towards Marsh Mills House, *c.* 1900. The man standing by the lock gates is probably the keeper himself.

The wooden bridge over the weir has been rebuilt but largely in the old style. The river weed now appears to be under better control.

ACKNOWLEDGEMENTS

Unless otherwise stated, the old photographs in this book are from the Oxfordshire County Council Photographic Archive, Central Library, Westgate, Oxford (tel. 01865 815432). The authors would like to thank Mary Busby of the *Henley Standard*, Mrs Foster of Moss Chemists, Mr Pete Goddard and staff at the Patisserie Franco-Belge, Mr Alfie Hay, Headmaster of Trinity C.of E. School, the Rev. Davis Pritchard and Jean Redwood of St Mary's Church, James Shawcross and staff at the Red Lion Hotel, Clare Sherriff and the Cretans Society, Sgt Dave Smith of the Thames Valley Constabulary, Mr Tony Verey of W.H. Brakspear and Sons Ltd, Henley Brewery, and Caroline Warburton, Press Officer of Henley Regatta.

Special thanks go to Mrs Hilary Fisher for kindly reading the proof text and supplying invaluable corrections and additional information, Mrs Jane Bowen, curator of the River and Rowing Museum, Dr Malcolm Graham, Head of Oxfordshire Studies, Oxford Central Library, Mr Derek Potts, Mrs V. Harris for all her help, and Carolyn Maunder at the Henley Centre for Local Studies in Henley Library. Any errors that remain are entirely the responsibility of the authors.

Readers interested in exploring further the history of the town and river are advised to visit the Henley Centre for Local Studies in Henley Library in Ravenscroft Road, and the River and Rowing Museum on Mill Meadows, which has specialist collections on the social and natural history of the River Thames and on the international sport of rowing as well as on the history of Henley.

A race has just finished in front of Phyllis Court, 1901. The timekeeper on board a steam launch checks his timepiece as crews from Kingston and Worcester College relax after completing their race for the Thames Cup.